Typophile Chap Book

New Series no. 3

By Jerry Kelly

with a Foreword

by Robert Bringhurst

Published by

The Typophiles

New York

About more alphabets

B	C	D	E
F	G	H	I
J	K	L	M
N	O	P	Q
R	S	T	U
V	W	X	Y

The types of Hermann Zapf

ISBN 978-0-9842744-0-6

CONTENTS

FOREWORD

✳

Letterforms are things that nearly all of us in the Western world have learned to take for granted. We treat them much like door knobs, water taps, thermostats, and hinges. We evidently think (in defiance of all logic) that what we read or write matters far more than how it's read or written, and that letterforms are just a way to get there, as a door knob is a way to open a door. At their best, though, letterforms are more like sailboats and cellos. They are works of art that beg to be used as well as admired. They make demands on those who use them; in return, they lend their beauty, strength, and character to the work for which they are used. As you read the page, the letters can vanish, reappear, and vanish again, depending where you focus your attention. But whether you pay them attention or not, they may have just as much effect on how you read as a sailboat can have on your experience of travel.

Hermann Zapf loves to compare typography and architecture: two domains in which the aim is to make room – exactly the right room – for things that have never happened before to happen. Zapf is one of history's greatest two-dimensional architects: magnificently skilled at making the right room on the page. When this is done, the words and the ideas that live there can flourish, and the eyes and minds that come there to visit can flourish as well. This process begins with the shaping of letters: those sweet little vessels of meaning that purport to have no meaning in themselves, and that you may not even see while you read what they say.

In China and Japan, where the public stature of calligraphy is higher, great calligraphers have been honored and remembered in the way great painters, composers, and poets are remembered in the West. The widespread use of computers is changing this now. Fewer people are writing with a brush; far more are writing with a keyboard. Appreciation for calligraphy and calligraphers is consequently fading into the realm of specialization. In America and Europe, where writing was mechanized long ago, the computer is having a slightly different effect, causing more people to notice that letters can change the way we read, and transposing at least a few of the names of type designers and typefaces from the realm of the arcane to the more mercurial domain of general knowledge. More people than ever before now know the names of Baskerville and Caslon, Garamond and Goudy. But it is not certain that more people have yet learned to see what there is to see, or to feel what there is to feel, in the shapes of letters. However much we take them for granted, they remain among the subtlest things we make and use. Hermann Zapf has made letters so subtle, so lovely they bring tears to knowledgeable eyes. And there are very few people who know Zapf's work as well as Jerry Kelly. Read him and weep. The shapes he shows us are a source of joy.

Robert Bringhurst

ACKNOWLEDGMENTS

⁕

David S. Rose & Paul Romaine of The Typophiles originally suggested publication of this book, based on a talk I gave to the Double Crown Club in London in November 2009; I am grateful to them for initiating the project and supporting it throughout the publication process. Thanks again to Paul Romaine, and to Robert Bringhurst, Nancy Leo-Kelly, Misha Beletsky, & Andrew Whitehead, for their invaluable suggestions to the text of this volume. Robert Bringhurst generously took time out from his busy schedule to write his lovely foreword, for which I am in his debt.

JK

ABOUT MORE ALPHABETS

On Hermann Zapf's ninetieth birthday we can look back on seventy years of exceptional type designs, for all composition methods, from metal type through digital character generation, all created to the highest standards of quality and usefulness. The Typophiles' first chapbook on Zapf's work, *About Alphabets* from 1960, dealt with most of his metal typefaces, while this volume of nearly five decades later considers a few of his major alphabet design projects since then, over a period of phenomenal change in the way letterforms are reproduced. Through all these eras Hermann Zapf has been a leader in producing exceptionally fine typefaces for various typesetting systems.

The well-known book designer Carl Zahn has summed up Hermann Zapf's unique combination of skills aptly: "His love of the beauty of type and calligraphy combined with an earlier ambition and talent in engineering: he is very much at home in the computer-oriented high tech that is America today. His openness and lack of pretense are particularly welcome in America. Hermann Zapf has fortunately inherited the great typographic and calligraphic traditions of Germany; but he has also a deep sensitivity to nature, the analytic mind of the scientist, a humanistic concern, and a hand blessed by God. These gifts he presses into the service of all mankind with an intensity that knows no waste." Those who are familiar with Zapf know these words to be true.

Zapf is justifiably well-known not only as a type designer, but also as one of the most important calligraphers of all time, and a most notable book designer and typographer. This book will concentrate mainly on his activities as a type designer.

Hermann Zapf has designed over 200 fonts – more than could possibly be covered in this small chapbook: if we devoted just a paragraph or two to each it would take several hundred pages just to touch on this body of work. Instead, this book will concentrate on several seminal types: not necessarily the most important – or most popular – of Zapf's fonts, but just a few that are somewhat representative of his work in the field of alphabet design.

Born in Nuremberg, Germany, on 8 November 1918, Hermann Zapf entered the world at an inauspicious time. Germany had recently been defeated in the First World War, and the reparations demanded by the allies as a result would cripple the country for many years to come – eventually contributing to the rise of Nazism. In addition, the Spanish influenza was sweeping Europe, taking millions of lives, including two of Hermann Zapf's siblings.
Zapf's background gives no clue to the origins of his superlative talent in the letter arts. His father worked in an automobile factory, but was dismissed from his job in 1933 because he was something of a union organizer, and the new powers wanted to purge such people – in addition to many others. Losing one's job with a family to support is never easy, but during the Great Depression such a calamity would prove even more daunting. Due the family's poor economic prospects the young Hermann Zapf could not continue his studies; he had hoped to

pursue a career as an electrical engineer (a field he would become involved in almost half a century later, when he became very concerned with the computerization of alphabet imaging). Instead he had to find a job and help support his family. Since he showed good aptitude for drawing, his teachers suggested he go into lithography, but potential employer's questions about political matters made it difficult for him to find a job. After ten months of searching he was finally able to secure an apprenticeship as a photo retoucher (not a lithographer, as he had originally intended) at Karl Ulrich & Company in Nuremberg.

In 1935 at the Norishalle Museum in Nuremberg there was a memorial exhibition of the work of the famous calligrapher and type designer Rudolf Koch (1876–1934), who had died the previous year (Koch, like Zapf, was born in Nuremberg). Upon seeing this show the sixteen-year-old Hermann Zapf became inspired to begin studying the art of calligraphy.

This was to be very beginning of Zapf's lifelong interest in letterforms. With what little pocket money the young Zapf had he bought the writing manuals of Koch (*Das Schreiben als Kunstligfertigkeit*) and Edward Johnston (*Writing and Illuminating, and Lettering* in the translation by Anna Simons, one of Johnston's earliest students), from which he began to teach himself the art of calligraphy. There were some wrong turns along the way, as is inevitable when one is self-taught: Zapf lost precious time when he mistakenly held his pen at the wrong angle to the paper, but once he corrected this error he progressed swiftly. So, in a very real sense, the very beginning of Zapf's work in the letter arts is directly attributable to the influence of Rudolf Koch, just as Koch's influence can be seen in Gilgengart, Zapf's first typeface design.

After finishing his apprenticeship in 1938 Zapf resigned from Ulrich and went to Frankfurt am Main to work with Paul Koch (1906–1945), the son of Rudolf Koch. The younger Koch ran a workshop that was involved in various graphic arts, with a particular specialty in the printing of music. It was called the Haus zum Fürsteneck after the medieval building the studio occupied (the house was destroyed by incendiary bombs during an air raid in March of 1944). This connection to musical notation led to two of Hermann Zapf's earliest typeface designs: Alkor (1939) and Musica (1942–43). Neither survived the war. His very first alphabet design, Gilgengart (1938), was cut and issued for sale, but only after a long and tortuous gestation, as we shall see shortly.

Zapf's career in type design can be divided into three periods: his early era, during the heyday of metal type, when his work at one of the largest type foundries in the world led to some of the most important fonts still in use today; his middle period, during the transition to different technologies such as photocomposition and digital character generation; and his later period (up to the present day), with important typefaces emanating from Zapf's hand, more than six decades after his first alphabet designs. A few typefaces that were never issued are also discussed below.

The elegance of the Gilgengart alphabet and the refinement of its drawing are already sophisticated and of the highest quality, even though Zapf was a mere nineteen years old when the basic

Gilgengart I abcdefghijklmnopqrſstuvwxyzttchcktzß
ABCDEFGHIJKLMNOPQRSTUVWXYZ
1234567890 1939-1940

abcdefghijklmnopqrſstuvwxyzttchcktzß Gilgengart II
ABCDEFGHIJKLMNOPQRSTUVWXYZ
1950-1952 1234567890

First and second versions of Gilgengart as shown in Zapf's first *Manuale Typographicum* (1954).

design was accepted by the Stempel typefoundry in 1938. The first book printed in Gilgengart was *Der Kaisers Neue Kleider* (Hans Christian Anderson's *The Emperor's New Clothes*), published in 1948. A few swash characters were issued with the font, but the large initial *V* at the beginning of the text and the extended swash *r* at the end of the book were drawn, and probably cut by hand by the punchcutter at the Stempel typefoundry, August Rosenberger, especially for this book.

The genesis Zapf's first typeface design was not easy. About ten years elapsed between the time the first drawings were made and the design was accepted for production until the release of the final font. Initially the design, with its thin hairline decorative strokes and slender proportions, was found to be a bit busy in the text sizes. So the entire type was re-cut, an extremely large and expensive undertaking in the era of metal type. Then, as work was proceeding on finalizing the typeface, the Nazi government decreed that black-letter types should no longer be used. It has been hypothesized that the Nazis felt their plan of world conquest would have been facilitated by adopting the roman typefaces, which are more familiar to the inhabitants of other countries.

Zapf himself was conscripted by the German army in 1940. After he, to put it mildly, showed a lack of skills needed for the infantry, he was transferred to a cartographic unit in occupied France. There he served the Third Reich by doing small lettering on maps (mainly for the invasion of Spain, which never occurred). Zapf used his considerable spare time drawing, painting, and practicing calligraphy. His work from this period include the drawings for *Das Blumen-ABC*, as well as three remarkable sketchbooks containing paintings and lettering exercises.

The revised Gilgengart type was finally released in 1952. A specimen from Zapf's first *Manuale Typographicum* shows the first and second versions of the design.

What influences might we find on the young Hermann Zapf that led to certain elements of his Gilgengart design? Clues abound in Zapf's earliest works: Zapf's second publication (after a text on William Morris) was *Feder und Stichel,* a display of 25 alphabets and quotations in oblong format, handcut in metal by August Rosenberger. There are some clear similarities to Rudolf Koch's *ABC Büchlein,* a showing of 24 calligraphic alphabets in oblong format drawn by Koch and Berthold Wolpe, and then handcut in wood and metal by Fritz Kredel and Gustav Eichenauer; but there are also significant differences. Both books are in the less common oblong format, both show assorted calligraphic styles from roman and script to uncial and black letter, in positive (black on white) as well as negative (white on black), and both were printed from expertly hand-cut plates. However, Zapf's designs are more finished and refined, both characteristics of his future work.

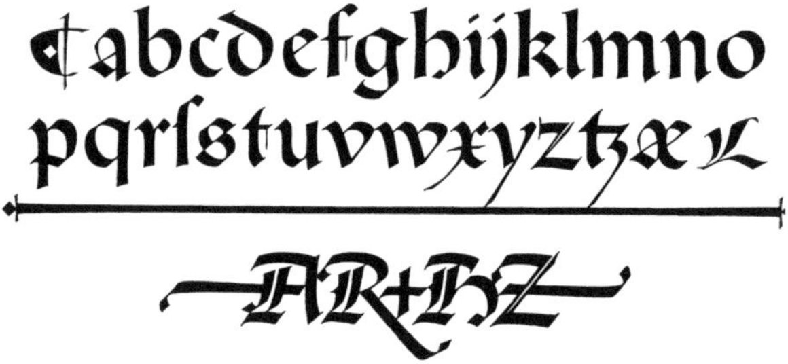

Rotunda calligraphy from *Feder und Stichel* by Hermann Zapf (written 1938–39; published 1950).

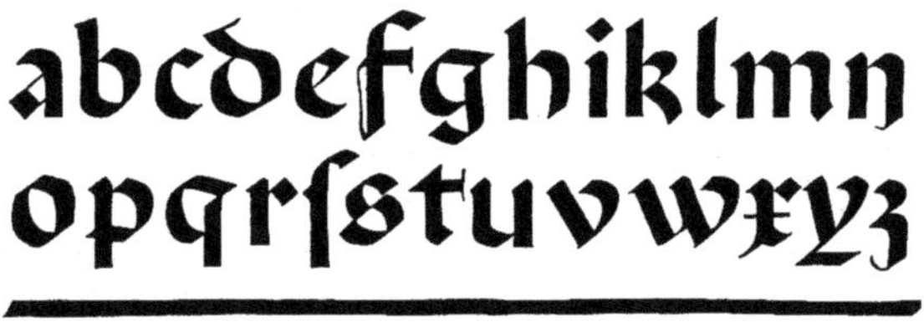

Rotunda calligraphy from *ABC-Büchlein* by Rudolf Koch (1934).

We should keep in mind that Rudolf Koch was capable of extremely refined work; however the *ABC Büchlein,* published in 1934, the last year of Koch's life, emanates from a period when Koch was more interested in a very direct and expressionistic style of calligraphy. Much (though certainly not all) of Koch's early work was far more finished.

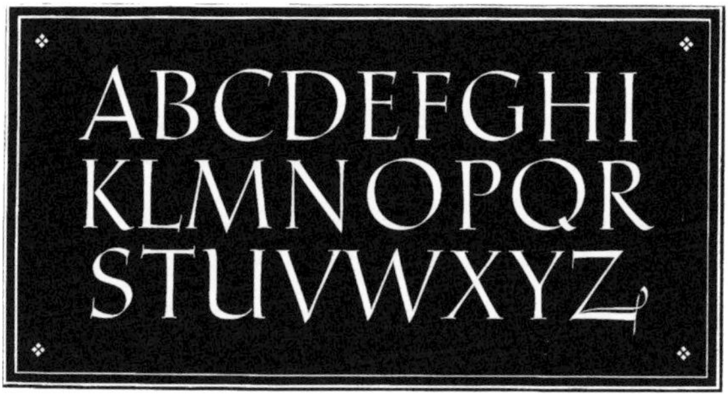

Roman capitals from *Feder und Stichel* by Hermann Zapf (written 1938–39; published 1950).

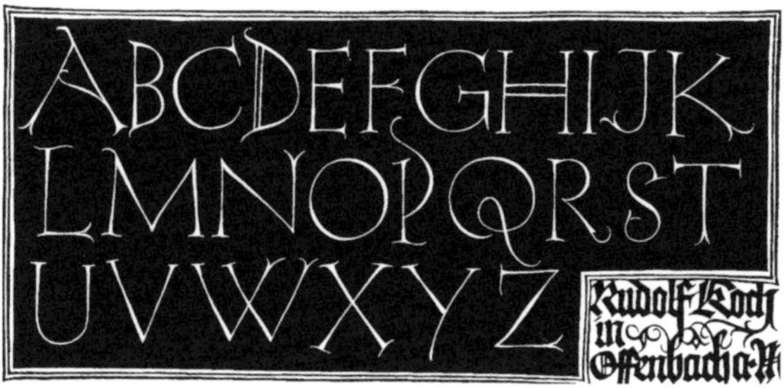

Roman capitals, also in white on a black background, from *ABC-Büchlein* by Rudolf Koch (1934).

Koch excelled in various approaches to calligraphy and letter design, from direct and expressive, to elegant and refined. We can see characteristics of the latter in the Wilhelm Klingsporschrift

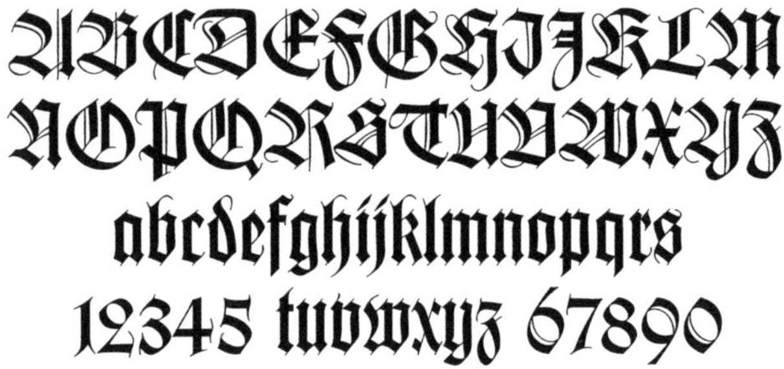

Wilhelm Klingsporschrift by Rudolf Koch, 1922.

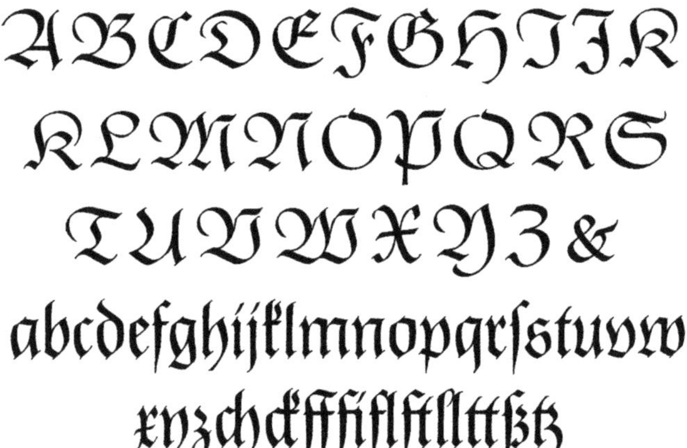

Gilgengart by Hermann Zapf, 1938–48

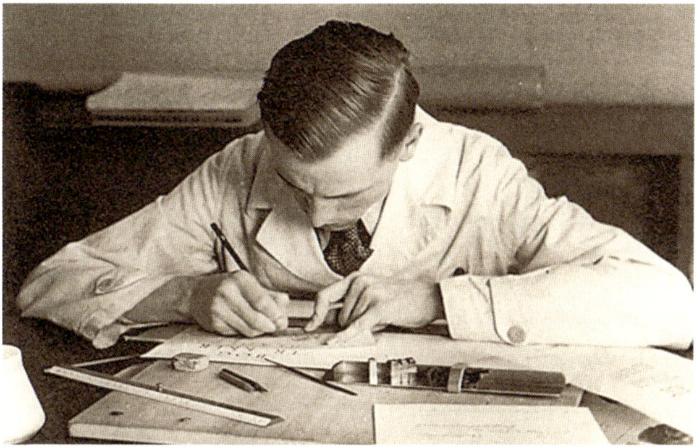

Hermann Zapf, c. 1938. Note the three letters in a type stick which he is drawing; see below.

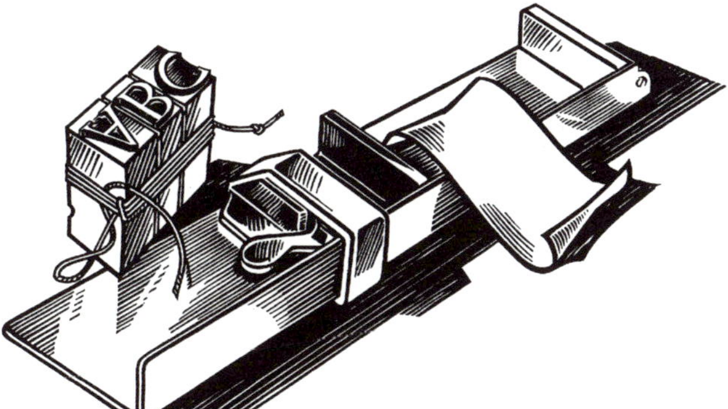

Drawing by Hermann Zapf, used in several type specimens beginning in the late 1930s.

typeface by Koch, a textura-style black letter typeface. Note the thin, decorative strokes emanating from junctures in the strokes, and the slight calligraphic swelling throughout the letters, so almost imperceptibly no line is perfectly straight – just as with pen-written letters. If you took these same principles, as displayed in Koch's Wilhelm Klingsporschrift, and applied them to a fraktur black letter design instead of a textura design, you might have the beginnings of Gilgengart. This is not to say that there is little of Zapf's hand in Gilgengart; there definitely is, and it could not have been drawn by Koch or anyone else, but many principles from Koch's type are at play here.

Zapf's second type design (not counting the now-lost music fonts) was a roman type called Novalis, which was cut but never commercially issued. It is not known if there is a single font of this type in existence today. Shown on the facing page is what may be the first proof of the type, from 1948 (this may be the only text ever printed in the type). Despite the headline, this specimen is not a text on "The Work of Rudolf Koch" as stated; it is instead actually written

THE WORK OF RUDOLF KOCH

In England, too, in the country which has produced such a highly gifted genius as the draughtsman Aubrey Beardsley, the circumstances are very similar. Here too in contrast to the sensuous art of France graphic talent predominates and has brought forth its most lovely flowers in the delicate ramifications of book art. We Germans know how much credit is due to England in the sphere of book art and letter design, and that it was there the movement started, in the 'eighties of the last century (if not, indeed, in some respects even earlier) that was to bring about a reformation in arts and crafts and pave the way for us all.

In 1891, when William Morris founded the Kelmscott Press, showing in its wonderful productions the artistic possibilities of the printed page, Germany was, unhappily, still manufacturing very mediocre books. However, the great moral energy spent by Morris in his efforts to raise the level of quality in all arts and crafts, and the genuinely religious zeal which gave impetus to his work, awakened Germany from slumber and released dormant forces. Germany also owes gratitude for much inspiration to the Doves Press founded at the end of the nineteenth century by Cobden-Sanderson and Emery Walker, whose aim it was to attain typographical perfection while avoiding ornament and illustration in their books, and who undoubtedly succeeded.

ABCDEFGHIJKLMNOPQRSTUVWXYZÄÖÜ

abcdefghijklmnopqrstuvwxyzäüößſʒchckffſifIſt& 1234567890

`1234567890.,-:;?![·]()»«"*†§¢áàôæœçÆŒÇ`

D. Stempel AG · 25.10.1948

Specimen of the Novalis typeface, 1948.

by Rudolf Koch *on* the work of William Morris. The mistake reveals a preoccupation with Koch. A bold and italic were also cut for Novalis, but work was put aside on this series to concentrate on a new alphabet design by Zapf, the typeface that would later become known as Palatino.

Palatino was the typeface that made Hermann Zapf's name preeminent in the world of type design. If Zapf had designed no other typefaces, Gilgengart (and, to a lesser degree, Novalis) would have gone down in typographic history as lovely, even excellent, designs that found little use. With Palatino typographers around the world became aware of Zapf's work. An early drawing from 1948 – amazingly over sixty years ago – has many of the essential elements of the design: a clear calligraphic ancestry tempered by typographic influences, slight swelling to the strokes, classical proportions combined with modern, open counters, etc. But with a closer look some of the details will seem strange: for example in the drawing the cap T, and lower case g in the roman, and the entire italic (except the italic capitals) all look significantly more cal-

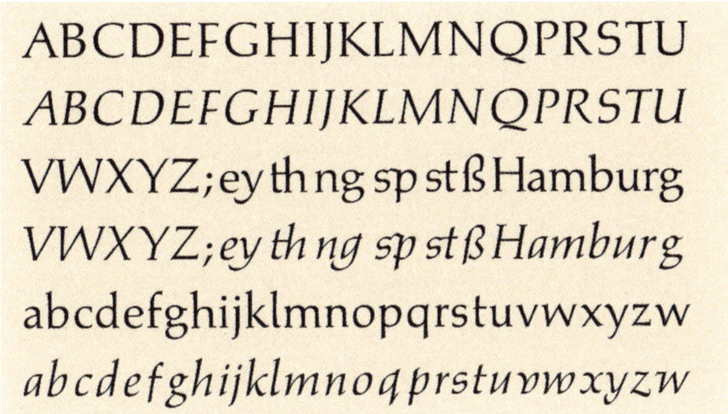

Original drawing for Palatino, 1948.

ligraphic and idiosyncratic than the final type. This drawing also shows finer serifs than those which were cut for the final type as issued in 1950. The design was produced without delicate thin strokes or fine serifs, which could present problems to printers when subjected to the stresses of everyday use on high-speed presses. With Palatino the Stempel typefoundry wanted to offer printers a new, modern-looking, generally useful Renaissance roman and italic font, which could be used to replace the older typefaces depleted during the war due to destruction or wear (lead was used mostly for ammunition, not type, between the late 1930s and 1945).

We can conjecture about how the changes may have developed for the Palatino typeface. Some of the revisions may have stemmed in a small part from the work done on the type by August Rosenberger, Stempel's punchcutter, as was common in those days. In the heyday of metal type manufacture the designer's drawings were often adapted "on the fly" by the punchcutter who cut the design in metal. With most of the fonts created during the first several centuries of metal typography, the type designer and punchcutter were the same person, as was the case with Garamond, Granjon, Van den Keere, Fleischmann, and others. For a few others such as John Baskerville, whose typefaces were cut by John Handy, and

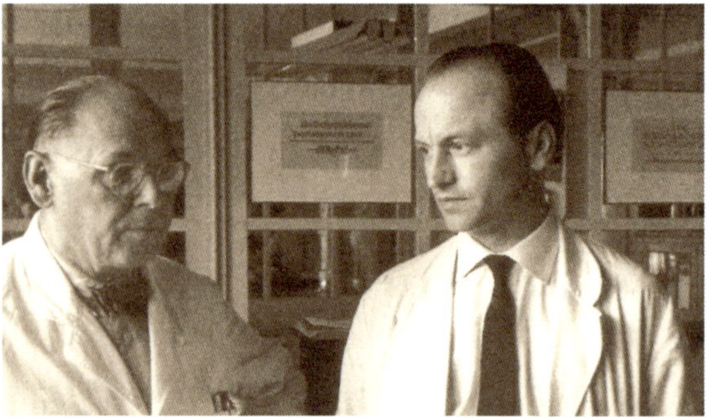

August Rosenberger and Hermann Zapf, c. 1951.

William Morris, whose alphabet designs were cut by Edward Prince, the designer and punchcutter were not the same person. In the twentieth century, however, the craftsman who cut the type in metal was rarely the artist who made the drawings (with the notable exception of Victor Hammer and one or two others).

Prior to Palatino, Rosenberger had worked on the meticulous handcutting of Zapf's calligraphy for the plates for *Feder und Stichel* (*Pen and Graver* in English), and cutting the pilot size of Zapf's Gilgengart font. The ties between Zapf and Rosenberger became closer with the cutting of this first of Zapf's type designs. The drawings made by Zapf for the Gilgengart type were un-

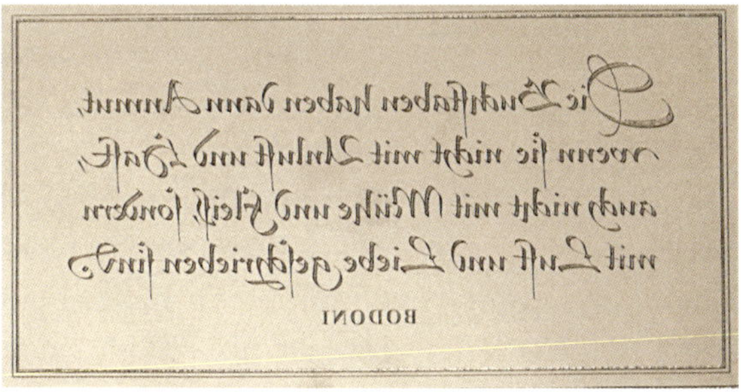

Metal plate for *Feder und Stichel (Pen and Graver)*, cut by August Rosenberger from Hermann Zapf's calligraphy, c. 1940.

usually finished, so the management at Stempel thought that with such complete drawings they could proceed directly to engraving matrices mechanically, without the intermediary step of punchcutting by hand. Zapf, however, insisted that the punchcutter Rosenberger be involved in cutting a pilot 36-point size. One can imagine Rosenberger's feelings in the matter.

Zapf acknowledged his debt to Rosenberger, possibly because at least some small part of the enormous success of the Palatino type may be attributable to miniscule changes Rosenberger made when cutting the punches. In 1996 Zapf wrote a book on Rosenberger, who had died in 1980. In it he described Rosenberger as "a man of unbelievable patience" for whom "no job was too complicated . . . I never wanted to cut punches or to engrave in metal once I saw the perfection of August Rosenberger's work."

The Palatino design eschews all influence of Zapf's early mentor, Rudolf Koch. Koch's work was always somewhat Teutonic in nature, but the Palatino design reveals no readily identifiable Germanic influence. Even though Palatino was drawn only a decade later than

Zapf's early Koch-influenced work, such as *Feder und Stichel* and Gilgengart, the type is more Italian than German, as the name implies. The Palatino family was eventually expanded to include two titling fonts named Michelangelo & Sistina, a lighter and narrower version for book work christened Aldus (with a special extra-narrow version), and italic swash capitals. These related fonts made Palatino the largest type family based on classic renaissance forms at the time. Today the character set has been expanded in Linotype Palatino nova to include a Greek and Cyrillic, as well as complete accents and unusual characters needed for nearly every western language.

Aldus is one of the most beautiful and all-around useful of Zapf's text type designs. It has the finer hairlines and serifs that were avoided in the Palatino design, and was drawn significantly narrower than Palatino, which has generous curves and counters. The narrower Aldus design was very useful to book printers, where every saving in the space needed to set the text would result in fewer pages, which would in turn translate into better economy – critical

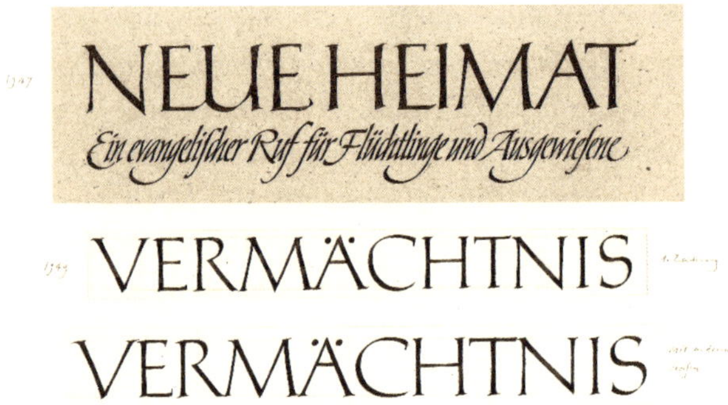

Early sketches for the Michelangelo typeface, c. 1950.

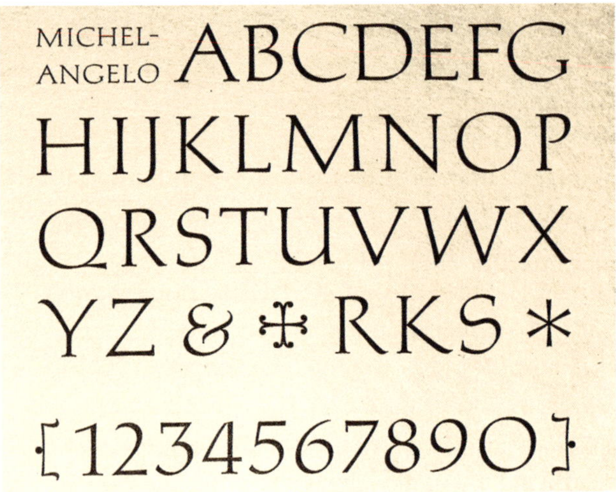

The Michelangelo titling typeface, 1950.

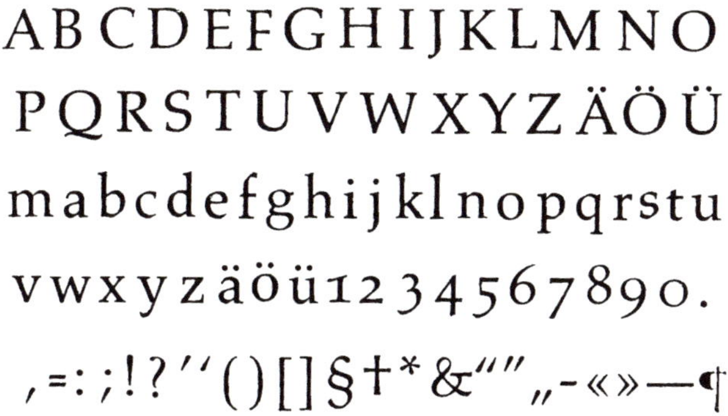

Proofs of the first trial cutting of the Aldus typeface (enlarged).

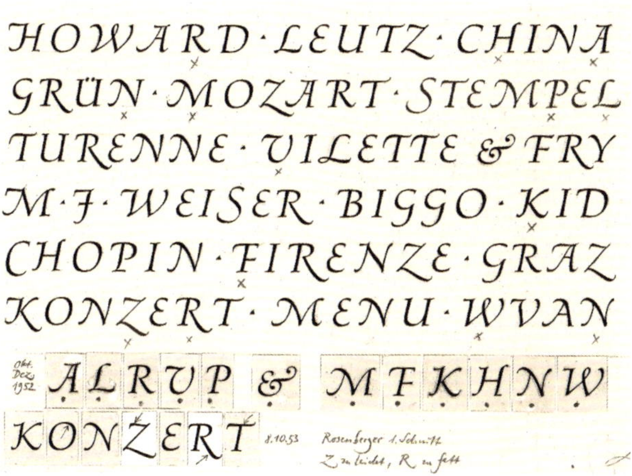

Drawing for Palatino swash capitals, with proofs of the first cutting pasted on, 1951.

to publishers dealing with lengthy texts; but not so important to advertising typography, where texts are brief. Therefore Aldus was ideally suited for book composition, and became extremely popular for such work in Germany, but barely made a dent in the book type market in the United States and elsewhere. With Linotype having a successful font like Palatino, the businessmen in the overseas offices decided not to promote Aldus, which might be seen as something of a competitor to Palatino, rather than a complement to it which, in point of fact, it was. Small caps and both old-style and lining figures were produced for Aldus, but the type was only cut up to 12-point Didot, even though Zapf made drawings for the larger sizes. Again, business interests ruled: the management of Stempel felt that Palatino would be adequate for sizes above 14-point, so the drawing Zapf made for the large sizes of Aldus was used only as a line-cut for one of a series of posters displaying Stempel typefaces (including individual posters for Palatino, Michelangelo, Sistina, and other Zapf designs) printed at Stempel in the 1960s.

Palatino became successful in Germany almost

from the start. Within a few years it also became one of the most popular new types in England and the United States. Sebastian Carter wrote in *Twentieth Century Type Designers* that "Palatino has proved so universally popular that its remarkable qualities tend to be taken for granted." Recently, Robert Bringhurst has documented over one hundred legitimate varieties of the Palatino design, ranging from the original roman and italic designs for metal types produced by the Stempel typefoundry and the Linotype Corporation, to the twenty-first century digital Palatino nova, re-drawn by Zapf with Akira Kobayashi for contemporary requirements. This list of more than a hundred varieties does not include any of the hundreds of illegitimate copies of Zapf's original. Palatino is likely the most copied typeface of all time, so if one were to count every version of Palatino ever offered for sale, it would probably total thousands.

The beauty and utility of the Palatino fonts were quickly recognized by type experts around the world. Even those of the "old guard," who were previously adherents of the revivalist style of typography prevalent in the first half of the twentieth century, saw the qualities evident in the Palatino type family, as well as the potential of the young designer of the font. No less an authority than Stanley Morison wrote the following to Dr. W. H. Cunz, the director of the Stempel typefoundry, upon receiving a copy of Stempel's publication *Almanach der Letternkunst 1951*: "I am glad to see specimens of fonts designed by Herr Zapf, in whose work, as I have already told you, I feel a deep interest" (letter of 6 March 1951, in the Cary Graphic Arts Collection, Rochester).

The Heraklit Greek font of 1953 is another member of the large Palatino type family. This type had a somewhat unusual origin: in the early 1950s the Insel publishing company wanted to print an edition of the writings of the Greek philosopher Heraclitus, so the art director, Gotthard de Beauclair, looked for a suitable Greek and roman font for the bilingual edition. At the time, in addition to his work as the head book designer at Insel, de Beauclair was also one of three art directors at the Stempel typefoundry (the other two were Zapf and Georg Kurt

Schauer). Zapf and de Beauclair collaborated on a number of book projects, including numerous binding designs for which Zapf drew the lettering. For the Insel edition of Heraclitus it was decided to set the German translation in Palatino, with the Greek text entirely handwritten by Zapf. These nineteen pages of calligraphic Greek text written by Zapf would later form the basis of the Heraklit typeface.

Zapf designed a number of non-latin fonts, including a couple of Cyrillic alphabets and an Arabic font (Alahram, from the Arabic word for pyramids), giving an indication not only of the aesthetic merit of Zapf's typefaces, but also of his enormous versatility. Stempel was a large company, and they had an international market, including some distributors in the Middle East. For that market Arabic fonts were needed. Zapf created one that an Iranian-born writer has told me she found difficult to believe was designed by someone born outside of a Persian-speaking country. He has also designed the Sequoya typeface (for the composition of the Cherokee language) for the University of Wisconsin and a Nigerian script for use in Africa.

εἰ μὴ ἥλιος ἦν, ἕνεκα τῶν ἄλλων ἄστρων εὐφρόνη ἂν ἦν.

ἥλιος γὰρ οὐχ ὑπερβήσεται μέτρα· εἰ δὲ μή, Ἐρινύες μιν Δίκης ἐπίκουροι ἐξευρήσουσιν.

...(περιόδους· ὧν ὁ ἥλιος ἐπιστάτης ὢν καὶ σκοπὸς ὁρίζειν καὶ ἀναβραβεύειν καὶ ἀναδεικνύναι καὶ ἀναφαίνειν μεταβολὰς καὶ) ὥρας αἳ πάντα φέρουσι.

κόσμον τόνδε, τὸν αὐτὸν ἁπάντων, οὔτε τις θεῶν οὔτε ἀνθρώπων ἐποίησεν, ἀλλ' ἦν ἀεὶ καὶ ἔστιν καὶ ἔσται, πῦρ ἀείζωον, ἁπτόμενον μέτρα καὶ ἀποσβεννύμενον μέτρα.

πυρὸς τροπαὶ πρῶτον θάλασσα, θαλάσσης δὲ τὸ μὲν ἥμισυ γῆ, τὸ δὲ ἥμισυ πρηστήρ... θάλασσα διαχέεται καὶ μετρέεται εἰς τὸν αὐτὸν λόγον, ὁκοῖος πρόσθεν ἦν ἢ γενέσθαι γῆ.

The Insel Verlag edition of the work of Heraclitus (Insel Bücherei no. 49).

Wenn nicht die Sonne wäre, würde trotz der üb=rigen Sterne Nacht sein.

Die Sonne wird nicht überschreiten ihre Maße; wenn aber doch, werden die Erinnyen, der Dike Helferinnen, sie dabei ertappen.

[Alles geht in kreisenden Umläufen; die Sonne als Leitgestirn läßt Perioden abgrenzen, Verände=rungen sichtbar werden und] die Horen, die alles bringen.

Diese Welt hier, die selbige aller Dinge, hat we=der einer der Götter noch einer der Menschen geschaffen, sondern sie war immer und ist und wird sein: immer=lebendiges Feuer, aufflammend nach Maßen und verlöschend nach Maßen.
Feuers Wandlungen sind zuerst Meer, des Meeres Wandlungen aber zur Hälfte Erde, zur Hälfte Kraterglut ... Meer löst sich auf nach Maßen des [die Welt durchwaltenden] Gesetzes zu dem, was es vorher war, ehe es Erde wurde.

The German text is in Palatino roman; the Greek was handwritten by Zapf and formed the basis for his Heraklit typeface.

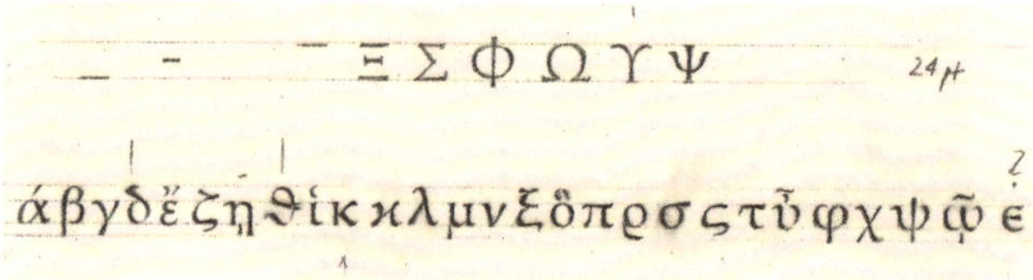

Drawing for the Heraklit Greek typeface, 1955.

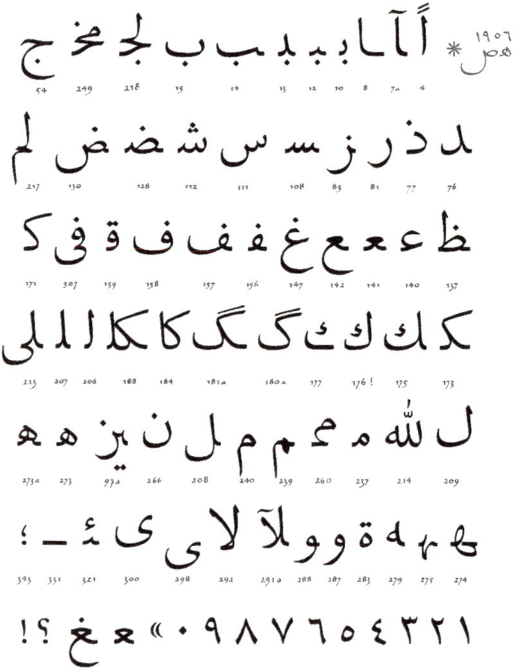

Drawing for the Alahram Arabic typeface, c. 1955.

Another early and popular metal type designed by Zapf for Stempel is Melior. Stempel had very close connections with the Linotype Company – in fact the Linotype matrices for Germany were manufactured at Stempel's plant. Linotype held a large share of the newspaper typesetting market (on the other hand, Monotype was used by a large percentage of book printers). With a proven young type designer like Zapf on their team Linotype would of course want a new newspaper font that might become a best-seller. That became the case with Zapf's Melior typeface. An early drawing shows some of the

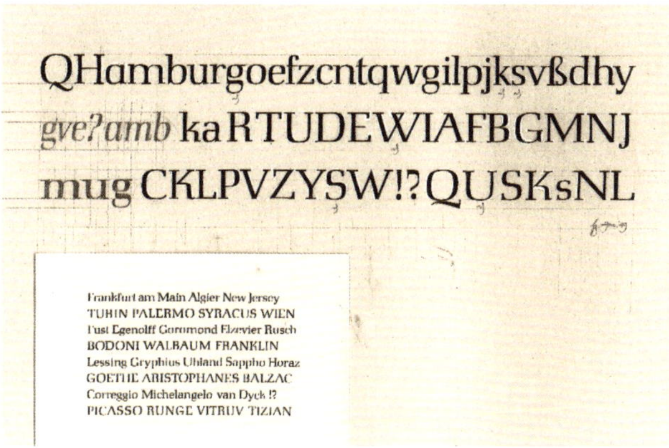

An early drawing for the Melior alphabet, ca. 1949

essential elements of Melior: the compressed forms, almost rectangular even for the round letters such as e and o (a shape called a "super ellipse": a cross between an ellipse and a rectangle), along with the large x-height that is crucial to the economics of newspaper publishing. But many other features, such as the thin hairlines and serifs, and the more unusual forms of a and y, would eventually be revised in the final design.

These designs, and several other handsome types, such as the Spencerian script Virtuosa and decorative Saphir capitals, bring us to the mid-1950s. Starting in the early 1950s Zapf began work on a novel new typeface, which at the time he was calling "Neu-Antiqua," or in English – contradictorily enough – "new old-style." To this day Zapf wishes that name had stuck, rather than the somewhat pretentious name given to the type by the Stempel sales department: Optima. Just about every typographer today is familiar with the design principles behind this enormously successful typeface. Optima is a "sans serif" design, but with thick and

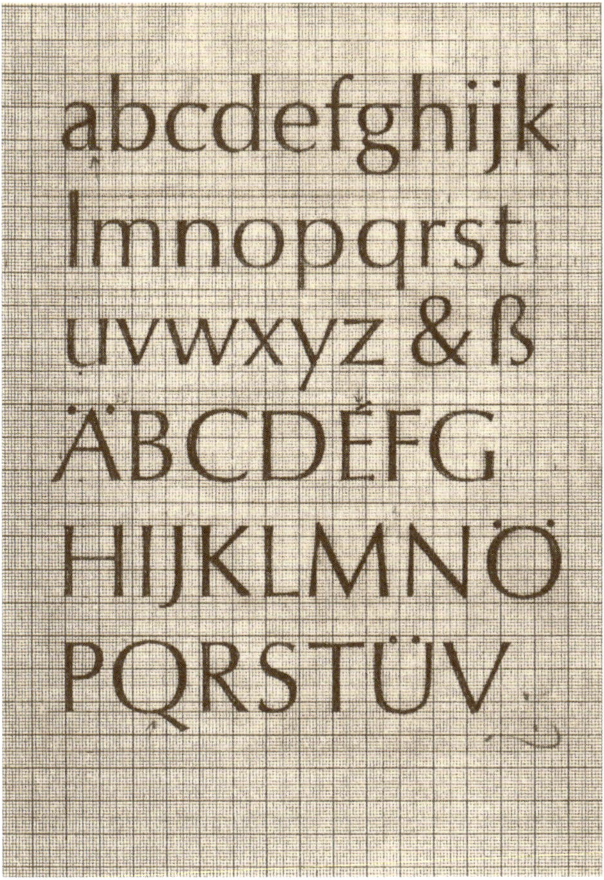

Pencil sketch for Optima, before the final ink drawing, c. 1958.

thin parts, unlike the optically monoline drawing of virtually all other sans serifs. The main strokes and endings are subtly tapered, lending an extremely elegant appearance, which is further enhanced by the perfectly classical proportions of both the capitals and lower case. All of these features make Optima a truly revolutionary design.

It was eight years between the time Zapf made his first sketches for Optima in 1950, and the type's release. While it might appear almost commonplace today, fifty years after its release, Optima's appearance in 1958 was momentous. In the fifty years since its release it has been almost impossible to improve on the design concept of this versatile serifless roman with stressed strokes. Today we see Optima everywhere, from letters cut in metal for signage on buildings to Chinese take-out menus. Like Palatino and other Zapf designs, it is a true classic.

After Optima only one more metal type, Hunt roman, was designed by Zapf and produced at Stempel. This brings us to the end of the first period of Zapf's work in type design, from roughly 1938 to 1960. However, before moving on to

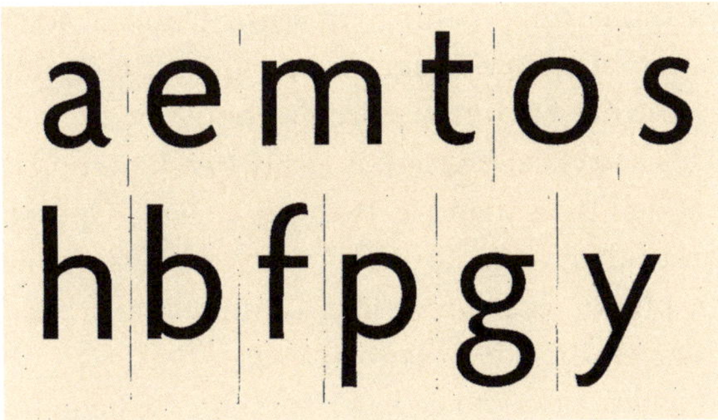

Drawing for Magnus Sans. Note the generous proportions of the descenders, a feature which would also appear in the Optima design.

the next era we can take a brief look at another Zapf alphabet: in the mid-1950s Zapf designed a sans serif, in the usual sense of the term: a serifless roman without any apparent thick and thin strokes. But this type, called Magnus Sans, was never issued. Many of the design's features were incorporated decades later in URW Grotesk, but Magnus itself was left on the drawing board.

The next period of Zapf's type design work is characterized by alphabets for new technologies. These can in turn be broken down into two groups: a] new designs created specifically or modern typesetting equipment; and b] adaptation of earlier designs made for metal casting to the newer computerized technologies.

This second sub-group is easily covered: modifications were made to Palatino, Melior, Optima, and other types to make them more suitable to photo-, and later, digital-composition. Such changes included the following:

1] some extension of letter parts to overhang (or kern, in the metal sense of the term), an aspect which was not possible in Linotype composition;

2] a slight "heavying up" of the design, particularly the thins and serifs, because in metal types these areas were drawn lighter, since they would gain a little weight through "ink squeeze" when the ink on the surface of the type was pressed into the paper. By contrast, in photo composition type actually lost a little weight when transferred to film, then plate, and then printed, so weight was added to compensate for these losses;

3] sharpening of the edges, again to compensate for deterioration during the photographic process; and

4] other changes, including taking the opportunity to revise some design elements which

Zapf had re-thought in the intervening years. Through such changes new versions of earlier types were released. Subtle modifications were made by Zapf to the authorized versions of Melior, Optima, and other typefaces from his metal type days. From a purely visual standpoint, of Zapf's earlier typeface designs, Palatino was the most changed when adapted for photocomposition.

When the first commercially viable photocomposition machines were released in the '50s and '60s, manufacturers were quite understandably eager to supply film versions of the most popular fonts to typesetters who purchased their equipment. At this time Palatino was one of the most popular fonts in the world, so every company wanted to offer it for their line to be competitive. Typesetting equipment manufacturers rushed to produce versions for their machines, often somewhat ineptly. Even the Linotype Company, which issued the original design in metal, re-drew Palatino in a not very sympathetic way; but for the Linofilm machine (which became widely used, especially in the United States), Zapf re-drew the type himself. As a consequence, practically every version of Palatino available today is actually quite far removed from the original metal design. A recent digital re-drawing of Palatino by Zapf with Akira Kobayashi, and its related family members Aldus, Sistina (now called "Imperial") and Michelangelo (now called "Palatino Titling"), has been issued by Linotype. This latest version includes a wide assortment of accented letters and non-latin characters, supported by Unicode, for composition in numerous languages.

Around 1960 Zapf was becoming increasingly frustrated with the appropriation of his type designs by other manufacturers without compensation. The new phototype technologies meant that virtually anyone with a camera and a little knowledge could easily copy an existing typeface (compared to the days of metal type, when extensive infrastructure was required for producing a new font, and associated costs were high). Whereas many European countries enacted legislation to protect type designers and other intellectual property, the United States did not.

On 15 October 1974 Zapf, along with several other members of the type industry (including

Aaron Burns of ITC), went to Washington, D.C. to present the case for typeface copyright protection before the Library of Congress. As part of his talk, Zapf summarized why typeface copying had become so pervasive in recent years: "You can copy [an alphabet] in two seconds with a camera. . . . Why should a designer spend years perfecting his skill in order to create a new alphabet only to have a cunning businessman take his design away overnight?

"During the time of type casting in metal (a period of over 500 years) it was not only an enormous investment for a type foundry to make a new alphabet and put the typeface on the market; also the unlawful copy of an alphabet was very expensive. Both sides had to invest a lot of money in the cutting of all the punches in each of the different sizes by hand. (A font in ten different sizes with all the accents is about 1500 characters. In 1963 Charles Peignot in Paris estimated the investment for 21 different weights of a type family at about 3,318,000 Ffr.)

"Protection of typefaces was always a problem. But in the old days this big investment of time and money served as some sort of protection."

By the 1960s this was no longer the case: phototype fonts could be produced with minimal investment. It would be staggering to calculate Zapf's loses due to this thievery. The result was that he became reluctant to continue designing fonts for type manufacturers, just to see his work quickly stolen by others.
Two companies in the United States worked to prevent such abuses: Hallmark Cards commissioned and copyrighted exclusive type designs for their corporate use, and later International Typeface Corporation (ITC), founded by Aaron Burns and several partners, came up with a new model for trademarking and licensing of typeface designs that proved quite successful. Both ITC and Hallmark commissioned typefaces from Hermann Zapf, by then indisputably one of the most important type designers of our time. The type designer and calligrapher Kris Holmes of Bigelow & Holmes wrote in 1980 that "ITC has credited its ethical practices as a primary reason that Hermann Zapf has returned to type design after abstaining for nearly a decade in protest against the widespread plagiarism of his designs."

These later fonts designed by Zapf for generation by camera and imagesetter, not casting in metal from matrices, required absolutely finished drawings. No longer would the design be influenced by the punchcutter or other intervention. Zapf's drawings for these newer, perhaps more unforgiving technologies, are superbly refined and finished.

Significant changes in the design and manufacture of fonts were brought about by the new technologies. No longer would punchcutters exert their subtle (and sometimes not so subtle) influence on the design of typefaces. The entire underlying principle of fonts changed, from metal letters impressed into paper; to black-and-white images lying on the surface of a sheet which had to go through a stage or two of photography, rasterizing, and then cathode-ray tube, and later laser generation. These differences in production would inevitably lead to changes in the "look" of alphabet designs. There was much to lament in the decline of the 500-year-old tradition of metal punches and cast type, but there were also new opportunities offered by sophisticated computer technologies. Nowhere are these opportunities more evident than in script typefaces, in which the kerning, overlapping, connecting, and the character set of fonts were severely limited in metal type. Granted, many types such as Granjon's civilité designs, Roger Excoffon's Mistral, and some other script fonts cast in metal overcame these limitations in remarkable ways, but even so a typeface such as Richard Lipton's Bickham script or Hermann Zapf's Zapfino would have been impossible to cut and cast in metal. Zapf himself has written about these changes from metal typefaces to photographic, and later digital, fonts:

"I have witnessed the steady change from traditional metal type to photocomposition. In all, it is a sad story, especially if your heart is closely allied with metal type, with an admiration for the work of the punchcutters and all the precision and unusual skill that is behind the casting of a typeface.

"... On the other hand, it is fascinating to watch the new developments, to discover the possibilities of the better conditions for designing new alphabets without the restrictions or limitations of metal types. Some people see the transition from metal to digital alphabets as a sign of dramatic decline, but we should not see this only from a negative point of view."

Not surprisingly, Zapf would soon take advantage of the possibilities offered by the new technologies to render calligraphic scripts in type. Jeanette Script (1967) was Zapf's first alphabet for Hallmark. The design was loosely based on the handwriting of Jeanette Lee, a secretary at Hallmark whose everyday cursive was considered exceptionally good, as well as typical of the best American handwriting. Other scripts for Hallmark would follow, such as Firenze (a Renaissance chancery) and Missouri (an upright calligraphic form). Noris (the Latin name for Nuremberg, Zapf's birthplace) and Venture are excellent scripts created for the Linofilm machine, but unfortunately they are rarely seen today.

Script alphabets designed by Hermann Zapf for newer technologies also include Zapf Chancery, which was one of the most successful of the fonts created by Zapf for ITC, and Zapfino script, one of the latest Zapf typefaces, and among the most popular fonts in use today.

Hallmark's typefaces were used mainly for their greeting cards, as well as for a series of books published for sale in their stores from the 1960s through the 1970s. Due to the nature of Hallmark's products, most of the types designed by Zapf for them are strikingly calligraphic, including the cursives Jeanette and Firenze, an uncial or two, and an excellent textura called, appropriately enough, Hallmark Textura. An exception to this calligraphic nature of the Hallmark alphabets is Crown roman and italic, which are more traditional text types which were used in several gift-book editions. Still, Crown does retain some calligraphic characteristics, together with vestiges of Hunt roman. Since these fonts were made for the exclusive use of Hallmark Cards and copyrighted, they are rarely seen nowadays.

Comenius, designed by Zapf for the Berthold Typefoundry in the 1970s, is another design not too dissimilar to Hunt and Crown. It is a very handsome and all-around useful design that I feel deserves wider use. The text of the present volume is set in Comenius. A somewhat condensed roman, Orion, was issued for general applications about the same time.

The International Typeface Corporation fonts were a very different story from the proprietary Hallmark fonts: ITC fonts were made specifically for wide distribution to typesetting shops, which some may remember as a thriving industry in the days before every designer got a computer on his or her desk and was able to set type themselves, instead of paying some other company for composition. While the United States government did not help with typeface copyright protection, you could trademark the name of any commercial product. ITC would register the names of its fonts, often including its corporate name and the designer's name into the official type name (such as "ITC Benguiat," "ITC Novarese," "ITC Veljovic," "ITC Zapf Dingbats," etc.). The result was that ITC fonts did not suffer the kind of rampant thievery seen elsewhere in the type industry. The company was paid royalties for the use of its designs by manufacturers of typesetting equipment, and ITC in turn paid fair royalties to the designers of the fonts sold, resulting in a substantial income for some successful letter artists such as Edward Benguiat (designer of ITC Tiffany, Souvenir, Korinna, Edwardian

Script, and many other alphabets for ITC) and Hermann Zapf.

Zapf's first font for ITC was Zapf Book, drawn from 1973–1975 and released in 1976. This alphabet design is a very crisp, neo-classical design in the Walbaum vein. The name is something of a misnomer since this alphabet, like virtually all ITC types, was made with an eye towards the advertising / display market; it was not intended for book composition.

Next came Zapf International, one of two typefaces which Zapf himself initiated, not as a commission from others (the other being Optima). Zapf International has a similar underlying structure to Zapf Book, but its rendering is entirely in the opposite direction: whereas Zapf Book has extremely sharp edges and ink traps that can hold up to the rigors of photographic character reproduction, with International Zapf has intentional over-round edges and curved junctures where strokes meet. In a way it takes the photographic distortion of letters and pushes it even further. These round interstices might also be seen as reflecting the natural effect of pen-written letters, where the ink pools slightly at the joins when it

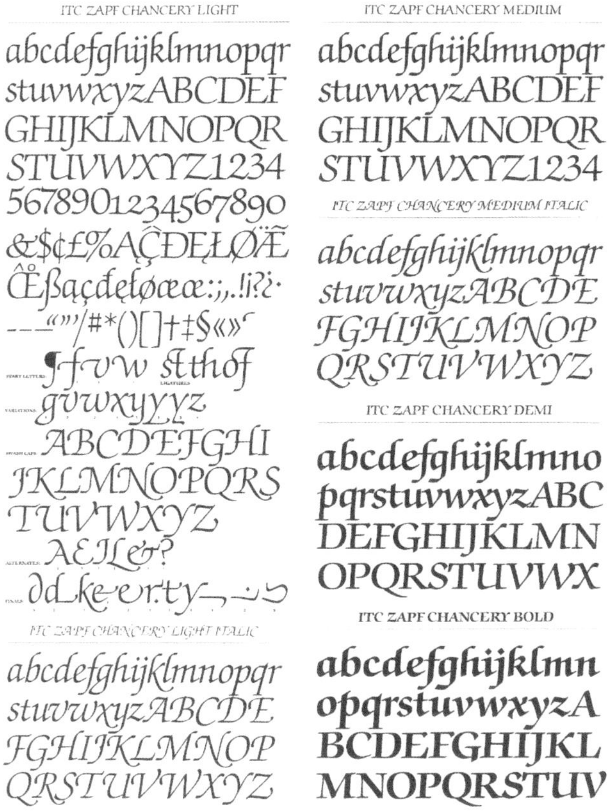

ITC Zapf Chancery, 1979. Note the almost upright and more sloped versions, as well as four weights and swash alternates.

is wet. Zapf International was released in 1977. It contains a special set of italic swash letters, in addition to the usual four weights of roman and four weights of italic required by ITC at the time: light, "book" or regular, bold, and extra bold (an assortment of weights that also is a tip of the hat to the advertising market; book designers have little need for such a range of weights).

One of the most popular Zapf designs for ITC was Zapf Chancery, issued in 1979. It was a suitable design for the period, with an unusually large number of alternate swash characters. Interestingly, it is quite different from Zapf's other italic designs, such as Palatino italic, Medici, or Firenze, all of which have more tapered strokes and a Renaissance feel.

Since in the 1970s and 1980s ITC would release all its alphabet designs in eight variations, an italic typeface such as ITC Zapf Chancery represented a problem: how do you create a roman for a chancery italic typeface? The decision was made to release Zapf Chancery in two versions, a somewhat upright design (inclined no more than 5°), as well as a more sloped variation;

each in four weights. Later ITC would abandon this policy in certain instances, with typefaces such as ITC Edwardian Script no longer being offered in an upright and sloped version with four weights each.

The initial drawing of Zapf Chancery is not what we see in the alphabet's design as issued: the original had finer hairlines and serifs. Unfortunately, one of the large composing machine manufacturers at the time, who was a major subscriber to ITC's alphabet offerings, required heavier thin strokes for technical reasons. Therefore the drawings had to be modified, resulting in a somewhat less elegant design; but it still proved to be a handsome and successful font.

One of the most important, yet overlooked, typeface designs from this middle period is Marconi, made for the Hell Digiset Company of Kiel, Germany. "Hell" may be a funny name to English speakers, but anyone involved in the printing industry would be familiar with Hell drum scanners, which were considered among the finest available. Hell was also a major firm in the field of newspaper printing. Much of this printing equipment was, by the early 1970s, incorporating digital technologies. It is a given to us today, but when Dr. Hell came up with the idea of storing fonts using digital code just about everyone thought he was crazy. Back then there was a real problem with achieving sufficient resolution to render curves at small sizes (a difficulty which would not be overcome for a decade or more), but the underlying principle was the way of the future. With hindsight this is easy to see today, but in 1965, when Dr. Hell introduced his revolutionary digital type composition equipment at a printing equipment exhibition in Paris, France, there was virtually no one who thought this could work in place of the then-prevalent phototype systems. However, one person involved with the type industry did see the potential of digital typesetting: Hermann Zapf. Unlike just about everyone else, Zapf felt digital composition had great potential, and he worked with Dr. Hell on a special font for the new typesetting technology. This resulted in Zapf creating Marconi, the very first alphabet designed specifically for digital character generation. Before Marconi all fonts for digital

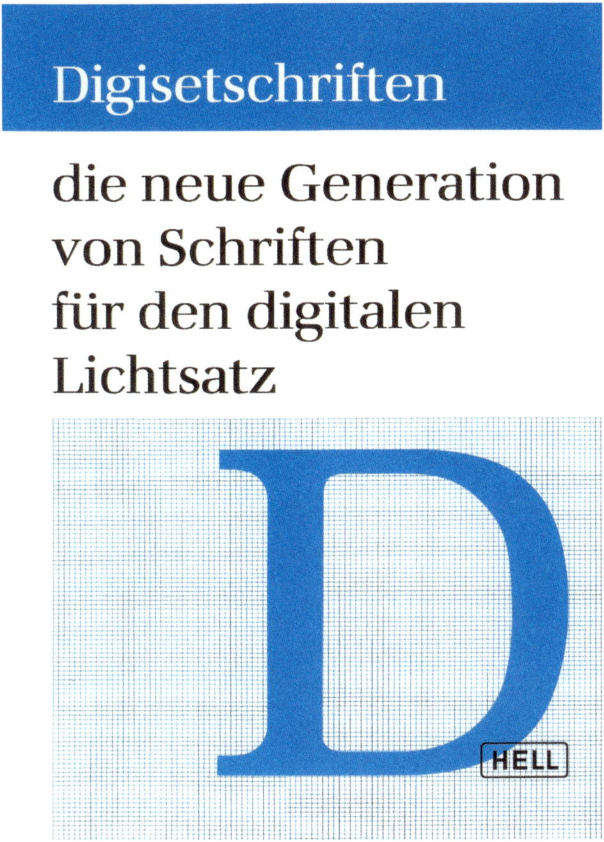

The Marconi roman, as shown in a specimen for the Hell Digiset system, 1976.

composition were adapted from earlier metal or phototype fonts.

For technical reasons noted above, Zapf incorporated as many straight edges as possible into Marconi. Despite such limitations, the Marconi font, with so many straight sides on the usually curved letterforms such as c, e, and o, and other constraints due to technical requirements, is actually quite an attractive design.

At this time (Marconi was designed beginning in 1973, and released in 1976), digital types had to be created by inking-in millions of squares on white board. The Ikarus system and other computer aids to type design would not be applied to alphabet design for years to come. Zapf's wife, Gudrun Zapf von Hesse, an accomplished letter artist in her own right, helped greatly with this painstaking task.

I feel that one cannot emphasize enough the importance of Hermann Zapf's Marconi alphabet design in the history of typography. The digital revolution in type and printing is now so firmly established that we can easily lose sight of significant innovations. The first font from nearly four decades ago designed specifically for this technology is a milestone in the 500-year-plus history of the mechanical multiplication of texts. Zapf also designed the Edison series as newspaper fonts for the Hell corporation. Edison was designed for maximum legibility in the small sizes used for newspaper text. It is amazingly readable in sizes as small as 6- or 7-point. In addition, Digiset Vario (a bold script for headlines) and Aurelia (a Venetian roman with italic) were designed by Zapf for Dr. Hell.

Another of the major typefaces from this period is the Zapf Renaissance series, designed for Scangraphic. The Renaissance roman and italic are among the most elegant and all-around useful of Zapf's later digital alphabet designs. A light and bold weight are available, as well as old-style figures, roman small caps, and swash alternates for the italic. Zapf Renaissance has classic forms, yet it imparts a contemporary look to text set in the font.

A paste-up made for study in developing the italic and its swash alternates reveals some of the origins of the design: the characters in this paste-up are taken from the lettering Zapf created in 1960 for his calligraphic rendering of a

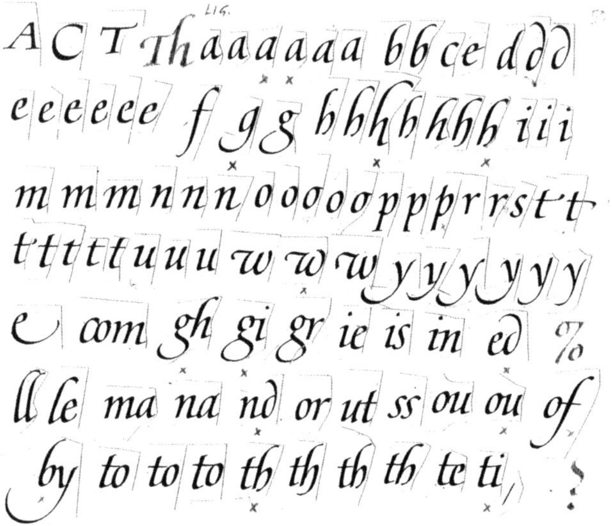

Paste-up of letterforms from Zapf's calligraphy for "The whole duty of calligraphy . . ." quote of Cobden-Sanderson, used as a study for the Zapf Renaissance italic design.

text from Thomas James Cobden-Sanderson's 1901 publication, *The Ideal Book*.

In the 1980s Zapf worked on a sophisticated computer program which improved the spacing and justification of type for exceptionally fine composition. This program was developed in cooperation with URW, of Hamburg, Germany, a company founded by Peter Karow. Karow was involved in various kinds of computer software, including the Ikarus program, which was originally devised for computer-aided ship design; but soon this system of ideal rendering of outlines through the use of Bezier curves showed its usefulness for other applications, such as graphic arts software, including computer-aided type design and Adobe's postscript language. The Zapf composition software, called the *hz-aesthetic program,* was eventually incorporated into Adobe's InDesign layout program, now the industry standard.

The third period of Zapf's career as a type designer is characterized by experimentation with unusual challenges in alphabet design. By the late 1970s Zapf's reputation as a type designer was secure, and through the efforts of ITC and the continued success of his types in Europe and other royalty-paying countries, Zapf's income made him, at last, a modestly wealthy man. He could now afford to pursue less remunerative projects. He became increasingly active in teaching, working at major institutions including the Technische Hochschule in his native Darmstadt, as well as the Rochester Institute of Technology and Stanford University in the United States.

Two unusual alphabets for obscure languages were designed by Zapf during this period: Pan Nigerian (1983) contains all the hundreds of special forms and diacriticals necessary for the nine primary languages spoken in Nigeria. Zapf did not charge a fee for the great amount of work involved in such a large character set (with several variants, including a monolined connecting script); instead he accepted a lovely African sculpture from the Nigerian authorities, which complements a twentieth-century figure by Gerhard Marcks in the courtyard of Zapf's house in Darmstadt, Germany.

In the late 1970s Professor Walter Hamady of the University of Wisconsin (and proprietor of the Perishable Press) asked Zapf to work on the designs for a Cherokee syllabary, again involving a large character set with many unusual forms. Once more the font took several years to finish, being completed in 1984.

At Stanford Zapf became associated with the

mathematician Donald Knuth. It was a fortuitous match: Knuth was one of the world's leading mathematicians, with a side interest in type design (he produced the MetaFont program and created an alphabet for his own mathematical books). Zapf was the world's leading type designer, who had wanted to be an engineer, and had a deep interest in mathematics since his youth. He has written:

"When I left school in the spring of 1933 [at the age of 14] my ambition was to become an electrical engineer. However, because of the new political conditions [with the Nazis rise to power], I was not allowed to attend the Ohm-Polytechnical Institute in Nuremberg. It was not until 30 years later that I was able to fulfill my dreams – when I became involved with computer technology in the United States."

Knuth was a leader in the American Mathematical Society (AMS), through which he sponsored a complex scientific font with a wide assortment of characters required for setting mathematical texts and equations. Such a font would need, aside from the usual Latin letters, punctuation, and figures, a Greek character set, a fraktur alphabet, and numerous special characters used in complex mathematical composition. Knuth wanted some evidence of handwriting to come across in the font design, since almost all mathematicians write equations by hand. Therefore, Zapf took the interesting approach of designing a simple, calligraphic letter, through which all of these various elements can be unified under the umbrella of the pen's influence. David Siegel, who played a key role in the development of Zapfino (see below) described the typeface in a Stanford publication from 1985:

"Knuth wanted a typeface that would be more distinguishable from text, yet familiar to mathematicians. He wanted letters that were consistent, but not dry. After all, his goal is to share the beauty and enjoyment of mathematics . . ."

A roman, script, fraktur, Greek, and occasionally even some Hebrew letters are used in mathematical equations. All of these assorted styles reveal the pen's influence in Zapf's Euler design. Interestingly, the numeral 0 has a special shape to instantly distinguish it from O.

At about the same time that Zapf was at work on this space-age digital font with a large character set for technical use, he was also designing an old-fashioned metal typeface in an archaic style for hand setting and letterpress printing. In the early 1970s the Michigan avocational typefounder Paul Hayden Duensing had the idea of reproducing a civilité-style alphabet, similar to one shown in Zapf's writing manual, *Pen & Graver*, as a new metal typeface. Not surprisingly Zapf felt that an entirely new design drawn specifically for casting as a metal printing type would be best. The result was Zapf Civilité, which is

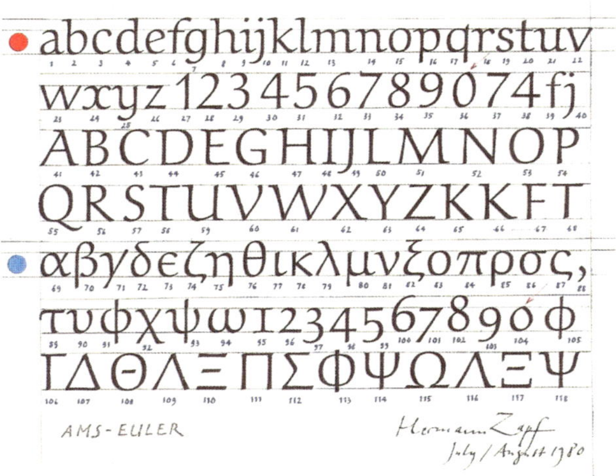

Drawing for AMS Euler, 1980 (issued 1986).

one of the most recent original metal type productions; coming out more than a decade after the last metal types were manufactured by large corporate entities such as the Stempel, Bauer, and Stephenson Blake typefoundries; none of which lasted beyond the 1980s. The first drawings for the cutting of the type in metal instantly revealed the beauty of the design. Upon seeing them in late 1971 Duensing wrote to Zapf:

"Dear Hermann;

"Your letter arrived yesterday and I hasten to reply to you promptly. I am delighted with the progress in the design and it also becomes more apparent each time why you are Der Weltmeister that you are! The swash letters are so beautiful they almost bring tears to my eyes! I want to cut them right now! . . . The figures are beautiful!"

It is interesting to note that Zapf had designed a civilité type for possible cutting by Stempel around 1940, but this lovely alphabet was one of the unreleased Zapf type designs.

The characteristics of the Zapf Civilité design as finally produced in metal were summed up nicely by Duensing himself: "In the Civilité of

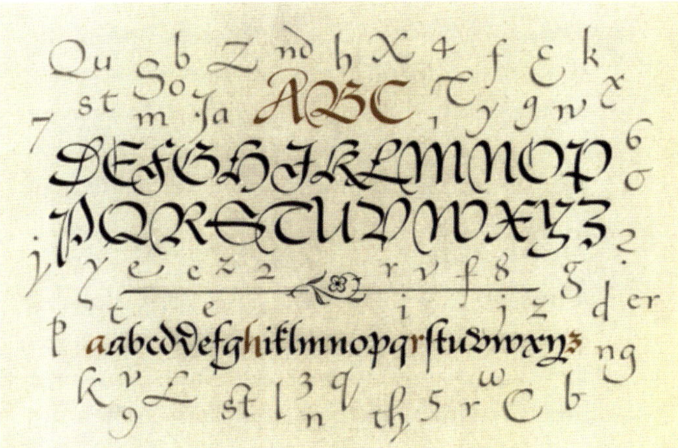

Early sketches for Zapf Civilité, drawn on a print from *Feder und Stichel*, c. 1977.

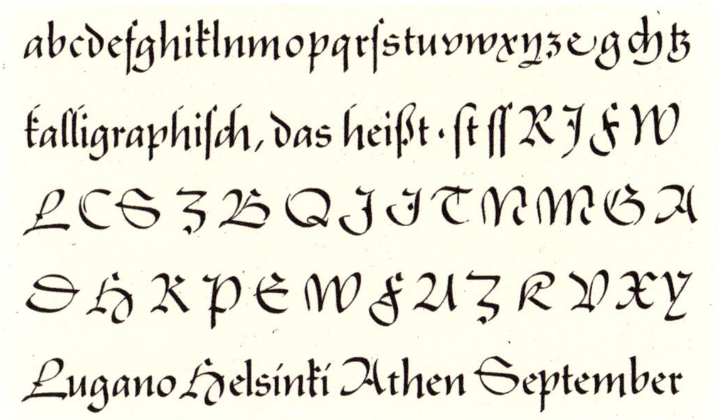

Drawing by Zapf for a Civilité typeface which was never issued, 1938.

Hermann Zapf, the designer has embodied the spirit of the historic letterform, while imparting a warm, contemporary feel to the individual letters. In general the counters are more open and there is a greater uniformity of letter width than in the historic model."

☆

A recent extremely successful Zapf alphabet design had a very unusual and circuitous history. We have mentioned that Zapf spent some time working with mathematicians at Stanford University in the 1970s. The students studying computer science there at the time were fascinated by the then-new concept of chaos theory.

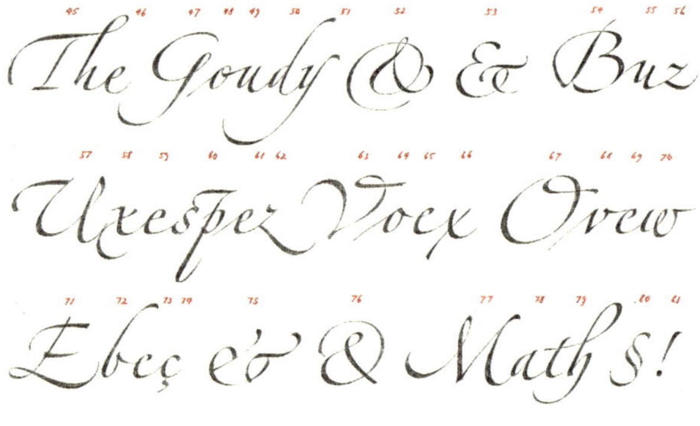

Drawing for Zapfino, c. 1977.

One such student at Stanford was a young man named David Siegel. Among many other ideas, he had the hypothesis that perhaps one might apply chaos theory to fonts. The thinking was that if you had lots of variant letterforms and contextual alternates you might be able to write a program somewhat arbitrarily (or chaotically) to apply this randomness to type composition, within some constraints, thereby truly approaching the infinite variety of handwriting. It is no surprise that Zapf would be interested in such an unusual project.

Like many of Zapf's designs, the work went on for many years. Along the way Siegel graduated Stanford and consulted for large computer companies, as well as starting a couple of his own. One start-up company he worked for at the beginning was a business called Pixar Studios, later famous as animators for Disney and other film studios. At one point he was making color cases for iMacs, before Apple started offering them in Blueberry, Mango, etc. Then Siegel saw the potential in the world wide web, so he wrote the first best-selling book on web site design, *Creating Killer Websites*. He also started a company making web page designs. For that company he hired the very talented Gino Lee, who himself had quite an interesting early involvement in the graphic arts: Lee printed by letterpress at his dormitory at Harvard, and also for John Kristensen's Firefly Press in Somerville, Massachusetts. In addition, Lee was an accomplished calligrapher. Eventually he wound up in California working for Siegel. As work progressed on this chaos theory type, Siegel had Gino spend almost all his time digitizing the thousands of letterforms needed for this typesetting system. Even with this combination of exceptional skill and effort committed to the chaos-type project, the program didn't catch on. In the end the vision exceeded the capabilities of the time, and the drawings, digitized forms, and computer programs languished. As David Siegel described it: "Market forces turned against us. We were able to build the fonts, and the engine worked great, the samples we made were splendid and the system should be a household name today. But the fonts were too expensive to build so the project was not economically viable. That is probably still true today. We could have sold it, but I would have lost too much money on it or at least taken much too big a chance, and the internet was booming and people were throwing money at me and Gino to design web sites for them. Thus, Zapfino and other handwriting projects took the back burner."

After some time Zapf did something quite uncharacteristic for him: he took it upon himself to show the design to Bruno Steinhart, then the director of Linotype in Bad-Homburg, Germany. Steinhart thought the designs might make for a good typeface. They took the thousands of characteristics and distilled them down to four variants of each letter (capital and lowercase), plus some additional swash characters and ligatures. Here is Zapf's summary:

"The basic concept at the start . . . [was that] no letter design should be repeated; up to six variants were available. In the Linotype version . . . we have only four variants to interchange manually without automating the process. But the very first idea of having a more individual and lively expression in composition was still our focus."

These original six fonts were released in 1998 as Linotype Zapfino. Like Palatino, Optima and

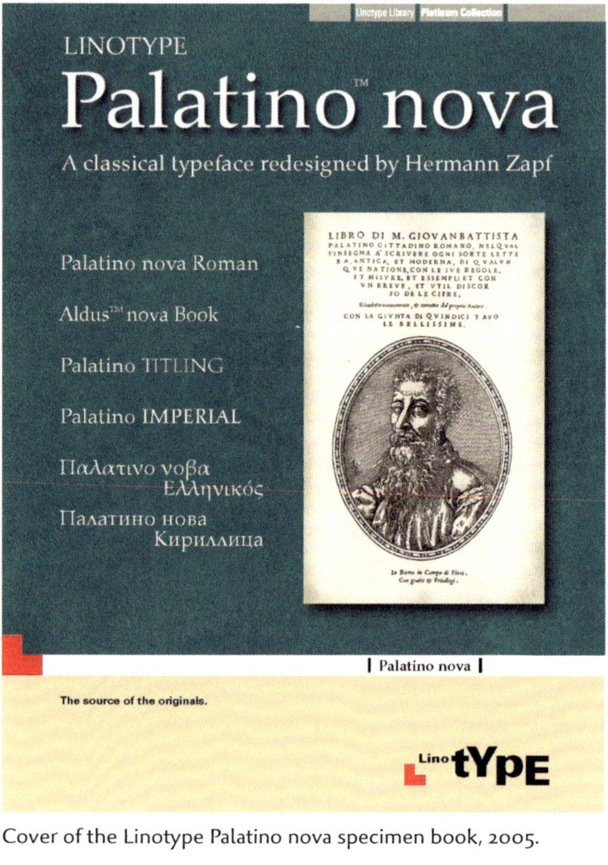

Cover of the Linotype Palatino nova specimen book, 2005.

ITC Zapf Chancery before it, Zapfino has been selected as one of the core fonts shipped with every Macintosh Computer – all this half a century after Zapf's first great commercial success, the Palatino type family. The rest is history: Linotype Zapfino has become one of the most ubiquitous typefaces today. Later it was expanded to include a bold & other features. Like all of Zapf's designs, not only has it proved universally accepted among the general public, but it is also admired by the experts in the field. With the advent of OpenType technology, a new version of Zapfino was released that combined variant letterforms in one font allowing for contextual substitution, along the lines of Siegel's earlier concept.

In the twenty-first century Zapf has concentrated on revising Palatino and his other earlier typefaces for modern typesetting systems. In the nascent days of computer-aided composition, when personal computers had only a few kilobytes of memory, the amount of memory available for font storage on PCs was severely limited. Today, with a few hundred gigabytes of memory becoming standard on even the most inexpensive machines, font software size is of little consequence. Therefore, extremely large character sets present no problem to modern computer hardware. The result is that many fonts today contain extended character sets, often including hundreds of accents, additional alphabets for Greek and Cyrillic composition, and alternate characters such as swash letters and numerous ligatures. Such large font sets were very difficult in metal type and with early computer-aided composition, but today Zapf has the opportunity to add such items to his popular alphabet designs. In addition, he has still further adapted these earlier typefaces for newer digital technology, above and beyond what had been done earlier for phototype systems. The Palatino nova font for Linotype contains not only updated drawings for Palatino, Palatino italic, Aldus, Aldus italic, Michelangelo (now called Palatino Titling) and Sistina (now Imperial), but also extended character sets for the roman and italic that include all characters necessary for composition in Greek, Cyrillic, and numerous other languages which require hundreds of special accents. The Optima nova series contains for the first time a cursive italic design, as opposed to the sloped-roman italic made for the metal version. Akira Kobayashi, who has collaborated with Zapf on much of this recent work for Linotype GmBH in Bad-Homburg, Germany, was instrumental in the drawing of this new italic for Optima.

The new italic design has a 15-degree slope, which is no problem in digital type generation; the earlier Optima italic had to be designed to duplex with the roman, on the same matrix and to the same width for Linotype metal casting, and thus had only a 12-degree slope. Also newly released are light, bold, and condensed variants of Optima, so that the Optima nova family is comprised of twenty alphabets.

Of exceptional note in the Optima nova series are small caps and old-style figures, which were never available in metal or phototype composition systems; as well as a handsome titling alphabet with many ligatures and alternate forms.

From the beginning Zapf would have liked to have small caps and old style figures available for Optima. One size of roman old style figures was cut in metal (you can see these in a trial cutting used for the back matter of Zapf's 1963 publication, *Typographic Variations* and his second *Manuale Typographicum* of 1968), but they were never released for sale. Small caps were never cut in metal for Optima, since Stempel's management did not believe that there was enough of a market to justify the expense of cutting and casting such supplementary fonts. This lack has been corrected with the Optima nova types.

The large character sets possible with modern digital fonts meant that additional unusual sorts could be offered, above and beyond the Zapf Dingbats issued by ITC in the 1970s, including new symbols that could not be foreseen in the '70s but are used today for web and other purposes. As a result, a large character set is included in the Zapf Essentials font issued by Linotype in 2001, containing a multitude of arrows, markers, and office signs, on top of numerous other symbols useful in typesetting.

☆

We can be quite certain that Hermann Zapf's place is secure in the history of type design, as one of its greatest practitioners of all time. Few in the future will equal, and none will surpass, his work in this field. The specimens on the following pages attest to his monumental output, but they are just a few dozen of the more than two hundred alphabets designed by Zapf for assorted technologies and purposes. And that does not even touch on his other work in calligraphy and book design, a truly phenomenal accomplishment in the history of graphic design.

We might also add a word or two about Zapf's character. His generosity and modesty are extraordinary. While, as Carl Zahn has written, Zapf uses his extreme gifts in "the service of all mankind with an intensity that knows no waste," he always seems to have time for any request from a friend or neophyte. All who know him have benefited from the association, and can bear witness to his kindness and consideration. Another characteristic of Zapf's personality is that he always shows the greatest respect for the work of other craftsmen, such as his early punchcutter, August Rosenberger, or the numerous printers with whom he has collaborated on various projects over the past half century or more. Hermann Zapf's numerous projects in the fields of calligraphy, type design, and typography are a lasting monument to his prodigious work in these specialized arts.

TYPE SPECIMENS

ABCDEFGHI
JKLMNOPQR
STUVWXYZ

*

NNSTTHTTQOO
OORQUWY

*

1234567890

❧ & ¶ * ⁜ & ❧

PALATINO NOVA TITLING

ABCDEFGHI
JKLMNOPQR
STUVWXYZ

*

abcdefghijklm
nopqrstuvwxyz

*

1234567890
1234567890

PALATINO NOVA ROMAN

ΑΒΓΔΕΖΗΘΙ
ΚΛΜΝΞΟΠΡΣ
ΤΥΦΧΨΩ

αβγδεζηθικλμν
ξοπρςστυφχψω

&ϐϑφϰ

PALATINO NOVA GREEK

АБВГДЕЖЗ
ИКЛМНОПРС
ТУФХЦЧШЪ

*

абгдежзиклмно
рстуфхцчщъ

*

ЉЊЋЏЩЬЭЮЯ
ыьэюяшвп

PALATINO NOVA CYRILLIC

ا ا ب ببب ت تتت ث ثثث ج ججج ح

ححح خ خخخ د د ذ ذ ر ر ز ز س ش

سسس ششش ص صصص ض ضضض

ط ططط ظ ظظظ ع ععع غ غغغ ف ففف

ق ققق ك ككك ل للل م ممم ن ننن ه

ه ههه و و ى سى ي ييي ٱ ٱ آ آ أ أ إ إ

لا لا لآ لآ لأ لأ لإ لإ ئ ئئئ ؤ ؤ ٹ ٹٹٹ

پ پپپ چ چچچ ڈ ڈ ڑ ڑ ژ ژ ڤ ڤڤڤ

ک ککک گ گگگ ں ں ی ییی ة ہ

*

١٢٣٤٥٦٧٨٩۷۴ ٠١٢٣۴۵۶٧٨٩

PALATINO NOVA ARABIC

ABCDEFGHI
JKLMNOPQR
STUVWXYZ

*

abcdefghijklm
nopqrstuvwxyz

*

1234567890
&

PALATINO NOVA SANS [REGULAR]

ABCDEFGHI
JKLMNOPQR
STUVWXYZ

*

abcdefghijklm
nopqrstuvwxyz

*

1234567890
&

OPTIMA NOVA ITALIC · OLD STYLE FIGURES

ABCDEFGHI
JKLMNOPQR
STUVWXYZ

*

AA LA CH DE EFT
ST HE LI VE KA LL ME
NN OO RE Q HR SA
TU NE TH TT Æ RA
& OO Œ QU

OPTIMA NOVA TITLING

ABCDEFGHI
JKLMNOPQR
STUVWXYZ

*

abcdefghijklm
nopqrstuvwxyz

*

1234567890
&

VENTURE

ABCDEFGHI
JKLMNOPQR
STUVWXYZ

*

abcdefghijklm
nopqrstuvwxyz

*

1234567890
&

NORIS

ABCDEFGHI
JKLMNOPQR
STUVWXYZ

*

abcdefghijklm
nopqrstuvwxyz

*

1234567890

MEDICI SCRIPT

ABCDEFGHI
JKLMNOPQR
STUVWXYZ

abcdefghijklmn
opqrstuvw&xyz
1234567890

HALLMARK TEXTURA

ABCDEFGHI
JKLMNOPQR
STUVWXYZ

*

abcdefghijklm
nopqrstuvwxyz

*

1234567890
&

MARCONI ITALIC

ABCDEFGHI
JKLMNOPQR
STUVWXYZ

*

abcdefghijklm
nopqrstuvwxyz

*

1234567890
&

MARCONI ROMAN

ABCDEFGHI
JKLMNOPQR
STUVWXYZ

*

abcdefghijklm
nopqrstuvwxyz

*

1234567890
&

ITC ZAPF INTERNATIONAL ITALIC

ABCDEFGHI
JKLMNOPQR
STUVWXYZ

*

abcdefghijklm
nopqrstuvwxyz

*

1234567890
&

ITC ZAPF INTERNATIONAL ROMAN

ABCDEFGHI
JKLMNOPQR
STUVWXYZ

*

abcdefghijkl
mnopqrstuv
wxyz

*

1234567890

ITC ZAPF INTERNATIONAL HEAVY

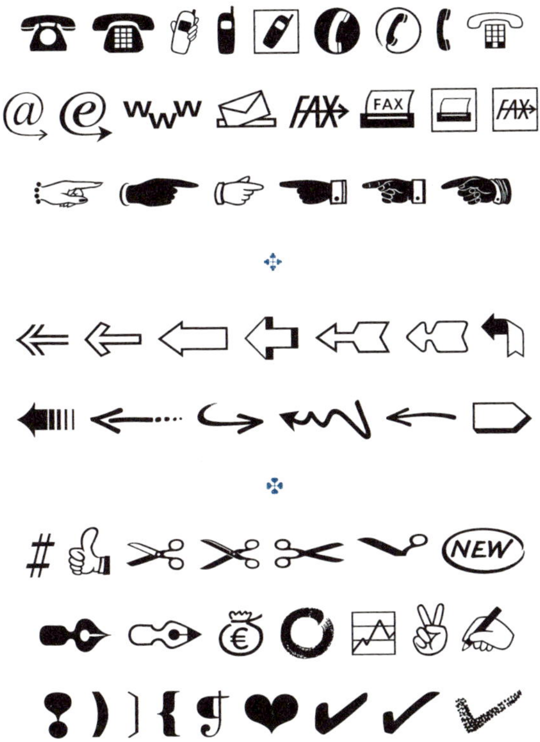

SELECTIONS FROM ZAPF ESSENTIALS

ABCDEFG
HIJKLMN
OPQRST
UVWXYZ

*

abcdefghijklmno
pqrstuvwxyz

*

b g f t d q y

LINOTYPE ZAPFINO ONE & "HYPERSWASHES"

A B C D E F G

H I J K L M N

O P Q R S T

U V W X Y Z

*

abcdefghijklmno

pqrstuvwxyz

*

1234567890

&

LINOTYPE ZAPFINO FOUR

ABCDEFGHI
JKLMNOPQR
STUVWXYZ

*

abcdefghijklm
nopqrstuvwxyz

*

1234567890

AURELIA ITALIC

ABCDEFGHI
JKLMNOPQR
STUVWXYZ

*

abcdefghijklm
nopqrstuvwxyz

*

1234567890

AURELIA ROMAN

ABCD
EFGHIJKLM
NOPQRSTU
VWXYZ

*

abcdefghijklm
nopqrstuvwxyz

*

1234567890

AMS EULER FRAKTUR BOLD

ABCDEFGHI
JKLMNOPQR
STUVWXYZ

*

abcdefghijklm
nopqrstuvwxyz

*

1234567890
A⁕Ω

AMS EULER TEXT

ABCDEFGHI
JKLMNOPQR
STUVWXYZ
&AGLNThkv

*

aemnt
bdfghijklopqur
suvwxyzz

*

1234567890

ZAPF RENAISSANCE ITALIC SWASH

ABCDEFGHI
JKLMNOPQR
STUVWXYZ

*

abcdefghijklm
nopqrstuvwxyz

*

1234567890
&

ZAPF RENAISSANCE ITALIC

ABCDEFGHI
JKLMNOPQR
STUVWXYZ

*

abcdefghijklm
nopqrstuvwxyz

*

1234567890
&

ITC ZAPF CHANCERY

A B C

D E F G H I J K L M

N O P Q R S T U V

W X Y Z

abcdefghijklmnopqur

stuvwxyz & b d g l ng th

» 1 2 3 4 5 6 7 8 9 0 «

δ·) sp r e n t a st y.

A B D D E H I K L P

& R S D

ZAPF CIVILITÉ

One thousand copies of this book
have been printed from Comenius
and other Hermann Zapf types.

Seventy-five copies are specially bound
& signed by the author, with additional
type specimens printed letterpress
at the Kelly-Winterton Press.

Printing by Capital Offset.
Design & typography
by Jerry Kelly.